D0810978

PUPS SPEAK UP

PUPS SPEAK UP

by Maxine Meltzer
illustrated by Karen L. Schmidt

Bonjour

Hello

Ni hou

Zdravstvuite

Hujambo

Shalom

Bradbury Press   New York
Maxwell Macmillan Canada   Toronto
Maxwell Macmillan International
New York   Oxford   Singapore   Sydney

The author and publisher gratefully acknowledge Berlitz Translation Services for their assistance in ensuring the accuracy of *Pups Speak Up*.

Bradbury Press
Macmillan Publishing Company
866 Third Avenue
New York, NY 10022

Maxwell Maxwell Canada, Inc.
1200 Eglinton Avenue East
Suite 200
Don Mills, Ontario M3C 3N1

Macmillan Publishing Company is part of the
Maxwell Communication Group of Companies.

The text of this book is set in Zapf International Medium.
The illustrations are rendered in watercolor.
Typography by Julie Y. Quan
Printed and bound in Singapore on recycled paper
First edition
10   9   8   7   6   5   4   3   2   1

LIBRARY OF CONGRESS CATALOGING-IN-PUBLICATION DATA
Meltzer, Maxine.
Pups speak up / by Maxine Meltzer ;
illustrated by Karen L. Schmidt.—1st ed.
p.   cm.
Summary: Dog characters in different countries introduce the words
for "hello" in the languages native to those countries.
ISBN: 0-02-766710-3
1. Polyglot glossaries, phrase books, etc.—Juvenile literature.
2. Salutations—Juvenile literature. [Polyglot glossaries, phrase
books, etc. 2. Salutations. 3. Vocabulary.] I. Schmidt, Karen, ill.
II. Title.
PB73.M45   1994
403—dc20   92-33687

Different dogs around the world greet their friends with different words.

"Hello" (he-LOH), says an American Chesapeake Bay retriever kicking a football.

Hello

A Brazilian Fila parading in a carnival
says, "Bom dia" (bohn DEE-ya).

A Hungarian komondor says, "Szervusz" (SER-voos) while cooking goulash.

"Hola" (OH-la), says a Mexican
Chihuahua from a busy marketplace.

An Irish setter plucks a harp and says,
"Dia dhuit" (DEE-a hweet).

From the top of Mount Fuji, a Japanese Akita says, "Konnichiwa" (KON-ni-chi-wah).

Riding the Tour de France, a French poodle says, "Bonjour" (bohn-ZHOOR).

From his horse-drawn sleigh, a
Russian borzoi says, "Zdravstvuite"
(ZDRAST-vui-tye).

"Hujambo" (hoo-DJAM-bo), says a
basenji in Zaire while shooting an okapi
(with a camera).

"Ni hou" (nee how), says a Chinese
Pekingese flying a dragon kite.

"Ahlan wa sahlan" (aha-LAHN wah saha-LAHN), says an Egyptian pharaoh dog headed toward an oasis.

Dancing the hora, an Israeli Canaan dog says, "Shalom" (sha-LOM).

Good-bye
(gud-BAI)

Chesapeake Bay retriever
United States of America

Tchau
(chow)

Fila
Brazil

Szervusz
(SER-voos)

komondor
Hungary

Hasta la vista
(AS-ta la VEE-sta)

Chihuahua
Mexico

Slán leat
(slon latt)

Irish setter
Ireland

Sayonara
(SAI-OH-nara)

Akita
Japan

Au revoir
(or VWAHR)

poodle
France

Do svidaniya
(doh svee-DAH-nya)

borzoi
Russia

Kwaheri
(kwa-HAIR-i)

basenji
Zaire

Zhai jian
(TSAI ji-EN)

Pekingese
China

Maha salamah
(mah 'a-sa-LAHM-ah)

pharoah dog
Egypt

Shalom
(sha-LOM)

Canaan dog
Israel

AUTHOR'S NOTE

I'd like to thank everyone who helped with this book, all my family, coworkers, friends, friends of friends, and the strangers, too. There's no substitute for hearing a language with one's own ears, so thank you for speaking to me.

Did you notice that Hungarian uses the same word for *hello* and *good-bye*? You can use it any time. Other languages seem a little more complicated. French *bonjour* means "good day." *Bonsoir* is used at night. The Japanese divide the day up even more finely. One greeting is used only in early morning, with a different word for late morning to afternoon, and another for evening. *Konnichiwa* is a more general way to say hello. The Irish have a different farewell for a person leaving or for a person staying. *Slan leat* is said to one leaving.

Most greetings and farewells have friendly meanings. The original implication of the Egyptian Arabic *Ahlan wa sahlan* is "you have reached your people and a fruitful plain," and the Israeli *Shalom* means "peace." I hope you find all that and more in your adventures learning about the people around you.